Candlemaking
Creative Designs and Techniques

Candlemaking
Creative Designs and Techniques

David Constable

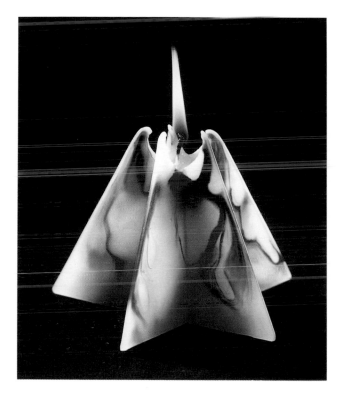

SEARCH PRESS

First published in Great Britain 1992
Search Press Limited,
Wellwood, North Farm Road,
Tunbridge Wells, Kent TN2 3DR

Black and white illustrations by Steve Pawsey

The author would like to thank Clint Twist for his help in the
preparation of this book; James Adams for his help in the
workshop; Brian and Lynne Steere of Clearlight Candles, Gayton,
Norfolk, for permission to use the dip and iron back candles
shown on pages 1 and 54, and the chunked candles shown on
page 40; Martin Newman of The Craft Shop, Greenwich, London,
for permission to use the landscape candle shown on page 37; Liz
Macaulay of Fly By Night Candles, Linton, Cambridge, for
permission to use the swirly chunked candle shown on page 38;
Ken Parsons of Spectrawax, Peebles, Scotland, for permission to
use the appliquéd candles shown on pages 47 and 50–1; John
Dennison and the late Bill Crawshaw for permission to use the
carved candle shown on page 53; Frances Fell, Dagenham, Essex,
for the original concept of the peeled banana candles shown on
page 60; Joe and Rita Tannetta of Candle Corner, Highcliffe,
Dorset, for permission to use the dip and carve candles shown on
pages 61–3; Werner Muhlenberg, Brunswick, Germany, for
permission to use the snake candles shown on pages 57 and 64–6;
Anne Collings of Candle Makers Supplies, London, for
permission to use the water candle shown on page 67; and Mick
O'Shea, Bristol, Avon, for permission to use the sand candles
shown on page 72.

ISBN 0 85532 683 2

If you have difficulty in obtaining any of the equipment or
materials mentioned in this book, then please write for
further information, either to the Publishers, Search Press
Ltd., Wellwood, North Farm Road, Tunbridge Wells, Kent
TN2 3DR, or to the author, David Constable, Candle
Makers Supplies, 28 Blythe Road, London W14

Composition by Genesis Typesetting, Rochester, Kent
Printed in Spain by Elkar S. Coop.

Contents

Introduction

For nearly the whole of recorded history, candles have been the main source of artificial light in northern and central Europe. Further south, where temperatures are higher, people have tended to use oil lamps because candles soften and bend in the heat. An oil lamp uses a wick with one end dipping into a container of liquid oil, whereas a candle uses a wick surrounded by a layer of solid fuel and, therefore, needs no separate container.

Until the nineteenth century, tallow was the main material used for making candles. Tallow is animal fat – usually obtained from sheep but also from pig and cow – that has been rendered down and partly purified. Suet, much used in traditional cooking recipes, is a very similar substance. Tallow candles give off greasy smoke and an unpleasant smell when burnt, but they had the advantage of being fairly cheap and reliable. In 1860, the scientist Michael Faraday demonstrated this at a public lecture, when he ignited some tallow candles that had been recovered from the hull of a wrecked ship. Despite having been submerged in salt water for fifty-seven years, the candles burnt steadily when lit.

Better quality, though more expensive, candles were made with different animal products, such as beeswax or spermaceti

An engraving made for the Universal Magazine *in 1749.*

obtained from the sperm whale. In fact, a spermaceti candle weighing about 75g (2¾oz) was made the basis of the standard 'candlepower' that was used to measure the strength of a light source.

Vegetable waxes have also been used, but in much lesser quantities. In China, wax was obtained from the seeds of the tallow-tree. In America, early settlers boiled up the berries of the bayberry bush and extracted wax from the residue. The desert shrub jojoba also yields a useful wax, and is now much in demand for 'natural' candles.

The first great improvement in materials came in the 1820s, when stearin was developed. Stearin is a chemical compound originally produced from refined fat, but now refined from palm-oil. It is harder than tallow at room temperature and produces much less smell. During the 1850s, paraffin waxes were first extracted from crude oil. The subsequent development of petrol-engined vehicles, and a vast industry to fuel them, has also ensured a steady supply of high grade candlemaking material.

The technology of candlemaking developed more quickly, and has remained virtually unchanged for the last five hundred years. The earliest candles consisted of a peeled rush dipped into liquid wax or tallow, and then allowed to harden. Such 'rush dips' were described by the Roman historian Pliny, and will have been familiar to countryfolk throughout northern and central Europe until quite recent times.

The candle mould was not invented until the fifteenth century, apparently in Paris, and could only be used for tallow candles, because beeswax could not at the time be cast in reusable moulds. Beeswax candles, destined for churches and the homes of the rich, continued to be made entirely by hand. The extra labour involved added to the already high cost of the better quality material.

Before the advent of gas lighting and electricity, the naked flame was a daily necessity if life was to continue after the sun went down. In Britain, there were no olive trees to provide oil, but there were plenty of sheep, and that meant plenty of mutton tallow. Two hundred years ago, every town in the country had at least one candlemaker or chandler. Their trade was tightly regulated by statute to prevent the sale of inferior candles and was subject to a tax on every candle sold. Not surprisingly, chandlers were often prosecuted, and imprisoned, for tax evasion. Also, making candles at home was forbidden by law and the penalties were quite severe.

It is hard to imagine the world as it was, when candles were so essential to civilized society that their manufacture and trade were legally controlled. Today, candlemaking at home is an enjoyable and relaxing hobby, non-essential but very desirable.

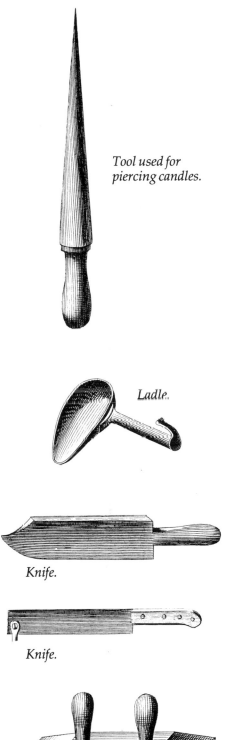

Tool used for piercing candles.

Ladle.

Knife.

Knife.

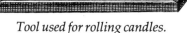

Tool used for rolling candles.

Equipment and materials

Equipment

None of the equipment needed for candlemaking is either expensive or complicated, and your kitchen probably contains some, if not most, of the bare essentials. Listed here are the items that you will need.

Thermometer

If you want to make good candles, then make sure that you have a thermometer. Waxes melt at particular temperatures, and

A selection of equipment used for candlemaking: thermometers; double boiler; dipping can; weighing scales; measuring jug; wicking needles; washing-up bowl.

remain liquid whilst they get much hotter, but their inner structure changes. It is impossible to guess the temperature of liquid wax and, therefore, the only way that you can be sure that you are working at the correct temperature, and get good results, is to use the right sort of thermometer. A clinical thermometer from the bathroom cabinet is of no use, as you need one that is calibrated between 38°C (100°F) and 180°C (356°F). A candy or cooking thermometer is ideal, and these are widely available from craft shops and kitchen-ware suppliers.

Double boiler

This should be made of stainless steel or aluminium, and the upper part should have a capacity of at least 3 litres (5¼pt). If necessary, then you can use one saucepan standing inside another, although this will result in uneven heating of the wax and you will have to take extra care in matching temperatures.

Dipping can

This is a tall cylindrical container used for holding liquid wax. Professional dipping cans are made of metal and have a wide rim so that they can be held in frames for multiple dipping.

Weighing scales

Ordinary kitchen scales are ideal for weighing materials.

Measuring flask or jug

This is needed for determining the capacity of a mould. Fill the mould with water, then pour it into the flask. For each 100cm³ (⅕pt) of water, allow 90g (3¼oz) of solid wax.

Wicking needles

These are steel needles 10–25cm (4–10in) long. They are very useful for inserting wicks and for securing the wick at the base of the mould.

Bowls

Washing-up bowls are ideal and you may need more than one. A bowl of hot water is used to keep dipping cans at the right temperature, whilst cold water is used as a water bath to speed up the cooling process.

Heat

You will need a source of heat for melting the wax. An ordinary domestic cooker (gas or electric) is ideal. Try to work as close as possible to your heat source, because wax loses heat quite quickly when it is carried about.

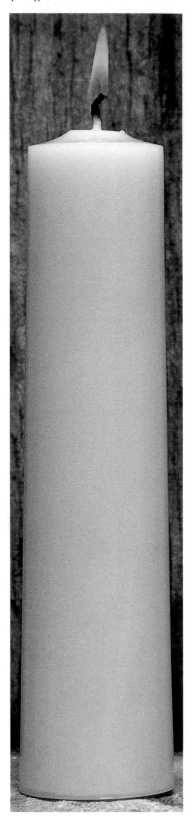

Candle made from a mixture of paraffin wax and stearin.

Materials

To make a candle you need wax and a wick. Both are available from craft shops and specialist suppliers. There is a range of waxes available, some of which have a variety of applications whilst others have very specific uses. Wicks are more straightforward, as they are all manufactured to an internationally recognized set of standard sizes. For making coloured or scented candles, specially prepared wax dyes and perfumes can be obtained.

Waxes

Paraffin waxes These are colourless, odourless waxes produced as a by-product of oil refining. They are all solid at normal room temperature and melt at temperatures between 40°C (104°F) and 71°C (160°F). The ones most suitable for candlemaking melt in the range 57–60°C (135–140°F). Paraffin waxes for candlemaking are available either in pure form, or with 10 per cent stearin already added.

Stearin This is a hardish white wax that is used mainly as an additive to paraffin wax to increase the amount of shrinkage in moulded candles. One great advantage of stearin is that the transformation from solid to liquid and back is almost instantaneous. There is no sticky in-between state. As a result, stearin makes a superb clear overdip that after twenty-four hours matures to a lovely crystalline finish.

Beeswax This is a wholly natural product available in bleached white or untreated shades of brown. Beeswax is quite expensive but has a beautiful aroma. It is normally used in combination with other waxes. Modern church candles contain 25 per cent beeswax. Added to paraffin wax in quantities as small as 1 per cent, beeswax will increase the burning time of a candle. If more than 10 per cent beeswax is used in a moulded candle, then a release agent must be applied to the mould beforehand.

Micro waxes Also a by-product of the petroleum industry, these are used as additives to alter the appearance and behaviour of paraffin wax. Micro soft is a tough, pliable wax that is the main ingredient of modelling wax. Micro hard is a brittle wax that is used in very small quantities (less than 1 per cent) to improve burning time and surface finish.

Overdipping wax A blend of waxes and resins, this is used to give candles a tough, shiny and opaque coating.

Water candle wax This is a specially blended wax for making exciting and expressive candles (see pages 74–5).

Dip and carve wax This is a blend of waxes specially formulated for use with this technique (see pages 58–66).

Plastic additive This is an opaque substance used in small quantities (5 per cent or less) to increase burning time and improve appearance. It has a high melting point and must be added slowly to wax at 104°C (219°F).

Vybar This is a proprietary additive used to increase the opacity of wax.

Wax glue This is a soft, sticky wax used to glue two pieces of wax together.

Mould seal This is a putty-like substance used to secure the wick in the mould and to prevent any leakage of molten wax.

A selection of materials used for candlemaking.
1. Dip and carve wax. 2. Water candle wax. 3. Paraffin wax.
4. Beeswax. 5. Stearin.
6. Beeswax chips. 7. Beeswax sheets. 8. Wax perfumes.
9. Micro hard wax. 10. Plastic additive. 11. Wicks in various sizes. 12. Overdipping wax.
13. Vybar. 14. Micro soft wax.
15. Mould seal. 16. Wax dyes.

Discs of wax dye.

Wicks

These are generally made of braided cotton and have been chemically treated to improve their burning characteristics. The wick is only a means to an end, as it is wax vapour that actually burns, the wick merely delivering the liquid wax to the flame.

The size of the wick is determined by the diameter of the finished candle. Wicks are available in 1.25cm (½ in) graduations. For paraffin wax, a 1.25cm (½ in) wick is suitable for a 1.25cm (½ in) candle, a 2.5cm (1in) wick for a 2.5cm (1in) candle, and so on. Beeswax is more viscous than paraffin wax, and beeswax candles therefore need a wick one size larger if ordinary wicks are to be used. Round wicks are best for beeswax candles and also for tall pillar candles made of paraffin wax.

Colours and perfumes

One of the great beauties of candlemaking is that wax can be dyed an infinite variety of shades and colours. You can use all sorts of substances to colour wax, such as crayons or poster paints. However, it is very important to use only wax-soluble substances. If other substances are used, then small particles will clog the wick of the candle causing it to sputter and go out.

Specially prepared wax dyes are the most convenient source of colours for candlemakers. These normally come in disc form for ease of division. Instructions for the proportion of dye to wax are supplied, but it is normally 20g (1 disc) to 2kg (4lb 6oz) of wax. For overdipping, dye should be used at four times normal strength. Do not be afraid to experiment with mixing dyes, or use them at strengths different from that recommended, but remember that wax dye only shows its true colour when the wax has cooled and hardened. When getting the right colour is crucial, mix a test batch the day before. If the colour is right, then you can melt down the wax and reuse it. If the colour is wrong, then you did the right thing by testing it. For really bright colours, paraffin wax needs the addition of a small amount of fat – beeswax and stearin both provide this. For pastel shades, 1 per cent of wax whitener should be used.

Wax pigments, which come in chip form, can also be used for colouring candles. Their main quality is that they do not fade, and they tend to be used for special techniques such as appliqué and dip and carve, as well as for adding final touches of colour to finished candles. As they are not wax-soluble, they should not be used to obtain a solid colour throughout a candle.

One of the advantages of paraffin wax is that it burns with hardly any smell. However, this does not have to be the case. A variety of special wax perfumes is available, and the best of these use natural fruit and flower essences. Essential oils can be used as an alternative to wax perfumes, although care is needed as some of them give off a nasty, bitter smell when burnt.

HOW TO BEGIN

Common sense with candles

FIRE SAFETY!

Wax should be treated like cooking oil. At temperatures below 100°C (212°F) it is fairly safe and it will not catch fire. At higher temperatures wax starts to vaporize and is then liable to catch fire. The exact temperature depends upon the type of wax being used. It is best to treat all wax above 100°C (212°F) as though it were highly flammable. If wax does catch fire:

- **Switch off the heat immediately. Do not move the pan.**
- **Do not try to put the fire out with water.**
- **Smother the flames with a damp cloth or metal lid.**

WORKSHOP WISDOM

Candlemaking is not an inherently messy occupation. This being said, upsets, minor and major, are bound to occur. However, with a little thought, most situations can be dealt with.

PREVENTION

- Wear old, comfortable clothes when making candles, and move or cover rugs and carpets. ● Make sure that you have enough room in which to work, and that all your equipment and materials are readily to hand. ● Remember that prolonged contact with hot molten wax will cause scalding. Do not leave pan handles sticking out from the cooker, and keep children and pets away from containers of hot wax. ● Do not pour liquid wax down a sink or drain, as when it cools it will set and form a blockage.

CURE

- Spills or drips of wax should be allowed to cool and harden before tackling the problem. ● For wax on clothing and carpets, scrape off what you can and then remove the residue by ironing through a sheet of absorbent paper (e.g. paper kitchen towel). Alternatively, you can send the item for dry-cleaning. ● For wax on wood, scrape off the excess and then polish the residue with a soft cloth. ● For wax on metal or plastic, immerse the item in hot water until the wax melts and floats to the surface. ● White spirit or turpentine can be used to dissolve small amounts of cold wax.

How to begin

I have always considered candlemaking to be rather like cookery. In both cases, a few simple techniques are combined to produce endless variety. Success in either field of endeavour depends upon the same critical factors; the right ingredients, accurate measurement, and precise control of temperature and timing. Equally important are liberal doses of patience and practice. The old proverb is true – practice does make perfect.

Melting wax and priming wicks are the two most essential skills in candlemaking, so it is worth taking time to become fully acquainted with them.

Working with heat

Most candlemaking, and virtually all of the candles described in this book, involve the use of molten, liquid wax. There are two ways of melting wax – a safe way and a less safe way.

The safe way is to use a double boiler, and for most candles this is perfectly adequate. The disadvantage of a double boiler is that it will not heat wax above the boiling-point of water, which is 100°C (212°F). However, a few of the candles described later in the book require wax to be heated above this temperature, and in these cases the wax must be heated in an open pan. Please be very careful when doing this and always heat wax gently. Monitor the temperature carefully and do not let the wax overheat.

Priming wicks

At the heart of every good candle is a good wick. If the wick is not right, then the finished candle will not burn correctly. You will always need a length of wick about 5cm (2in) longer than the candle you are making. If in doubt then be generous, as an overlong wick can always be trimmed. The instructions for each candle will tell you what grade of wick to use.

How to – priming wicks

EQUIPMENT AND MATERIALS
Double boiler; thermometer; grease-proof paper in a baking tray; nail; 1kg (2lb 3oz) paraffin wax; three 60cm (24in) lengths of 1.25cm (½in) wick.

METHOD
1. Heat the wax gently until it reaches 71°C (160°F), then switch off the heat.

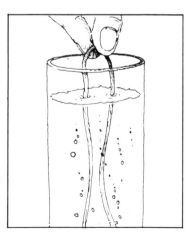

Priming the wick.

2. Fold a length of wick in half and, holding it by the middle, dip it into the molten wax for one minute. This forces out any air or moisture. Leave the thermometer in the wax whilst you work and note how long the wax holds its temperature. This will give you some idea of how often you need to re-heat wax when working at a constant temperature.

3. Remove the pair of wicks and straighten them with your fingers.

4. Hang the wicks over a nail to cool.

5. Whilst it is still liquid, pour the wax on to sheets of grease-proof paper to cool. When it has solidified it can be stored for later use.

Dipping

The simplest method of making a candle is to repeat the wick priming process over and over again. By repeatedly dipping the wick into the molten wax, you can build up a candle to any thickness you want. Dipped candles have a characteristic tapering shape, hence the name 'tapers' for candles made in this way.

For ease of handling, candles are usually dipped in pairs and are separated only when they have cooled completely. When hanging dipped candles to cool, make sure that they do not touch each other whilst the surface layers are still sticky. Hanging them over two nails, rather than just one, is an easy way to keep them apart.

How to – dipped candles

EQUIPMENT AND MATERIALS
Large saucepan; thermometer; metal dipping can at least 30cm (12in) tall; knife; 3kg (6lb 10oz) paraffin wax; three 60cm (24in) lengths of 1.25cm (½in) wick; 60g (approx. 3 discs) red dye. These materials are sufficient to make six coloured table candles, each 25cm (10in) tall and 1.2–1.9cm (½–¾in) in diameter.

METHOD
1. Put the chunks of wax into the dipping can, then stand the can in a saucepan half full of water. Heat the water until the wax melts and the temperature reaches 71°C (160°F), and then turn the heat right down. Remember to measure the temperature of the liquid wax, not the water. If you are not using wicks that you have already prepared, then prime them now (see page 15).

2. Add the red dye to the wax until you achieve a good colour. Be careful not to use too much.

3. Check that the temperature of the wax is still 71°C (160°F), then dip each pair of wicks into the wax for about three seconds, and allow them to cool for one to four minutes depending upon the room temperature.

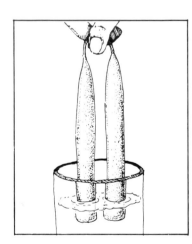

Dipping the candles.

Opposite: *a selection of dipped candles.*

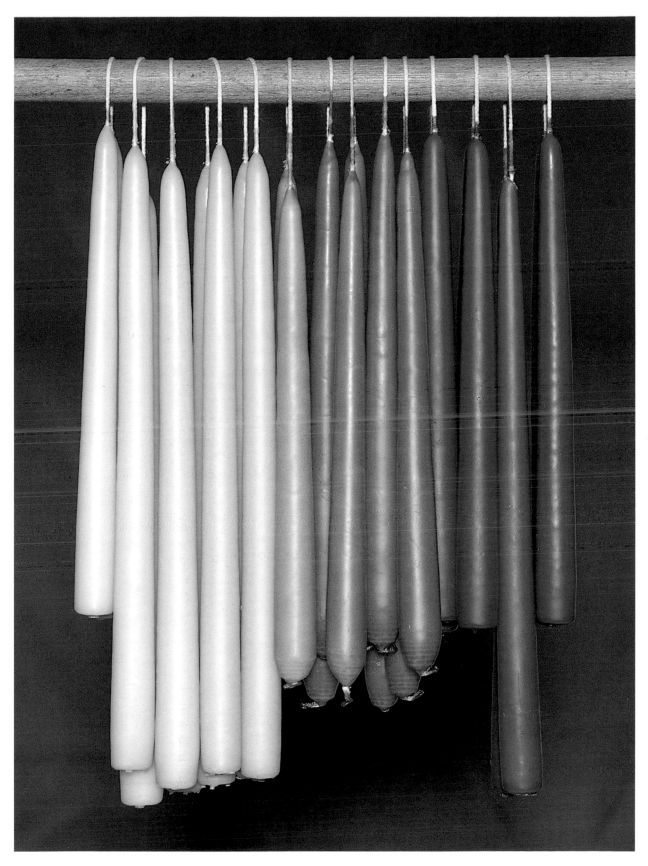

4. Repeat this process until the candles are the desired thickness.

5. Switch up the heat and raise the temperature of the wax to 82°C (180°F).

6. Give each pair of candles a final three-second dip, and allow them to cool for about three minutes. This final coating in hotter wax gives the candles a lovely smooth finish.

7. Trim the bases flat with a knife, taking care not to spoil the smooth finish with fingerprints. Allow the candles to cool for one hour.

If you find that dipping produces a lumpy surface, then it means that your wax is too cold, so re-heat it to the correct temperature. Whilst the candles are still soft, roll them against a work surface to flatten the lumps before dipping them again.

More about dipping

Home-made dipped candles are extremely attractive and have a special quality that factory-made candles just cannot match. There may be occasions when you want to produce dipped candles in quantity, e.g. to decorate the tables at a wedding feast, or to give as presents. Dipping them in pairs can be a laborious task, and with a little more preparation multiple dipping can speed up the process considerably.

Candles can be dipped in quantity by tying pairs of wicks to a frame. The only restriction on numbers is the diameter of the dipping can that you have available. The frame can be a simple rod, a hoop, or a square. Metal baking grids are especially useful to the home dipper. There are two important points to remember. Firstly, when tying the wicks on, make sure that you leave enough room between them to accommodate the finished candles – three candle diameters between wicks is about right. Secondly, do not forget that a frame of completed candles is a lot heavier than a frame of wicks.

Overdipping

Dramatic effects can be obtained by overdipping completed candles with wax of a strongly contrasting colour. The contrast is only revealed when the candle is lit.

How to – overdipping (blue on white)

EQUIPMENT AND MATERIALS

Large saucepan; thermometer; dipping can; some white dipped candles; 2kg (4lb 6oz) paraffin wax; 40g (approx. 2 discs) blue dye.

METHOD

1. Heat the wax in the dipping can to 82°C (180°F) and add dye to make a strong blue colour.

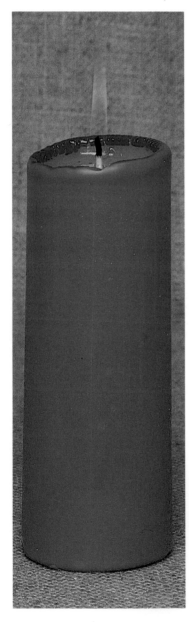

Overdipped candle in blue and white.

2. Dip the candles into the wax two or three times, leaving about thirty seconds between dips. If your candles do not pick up much colour, then your wax is too hot. If the coloured coating is scaly, then your wax is too cold. In both cases, check and adjust the temperature before continuing.

Hand finishing

Freshly dipped candles can be worked by hand whilst they are still warm and soft. You can test if they are soft enough – the candle should bend easily into an S shape. If they have become too hard, then candles can be softened by dipping them into wax at 71°C (160°F) for about three seconds. You must then wait thirty seconds for the surface to cool before starting work. Wax will not stick to water, so when handling warm wax it helps to keep your hands, rolling-pin, work surface, etc., wet.

Plaited candles are very attractive, but do not use candles to teach yourself to plait. If you are not sure, then practise with bits of string. Even so, plaiting is often much easier with two people.

Plaited candles in orange, green, and white.

How to – plaited candles

EQUIPMENT AND MATERIALS

Scissors; a hook at a convenient working height; two pairs of freshly made candles about 1.25cm (½in) in diameter and at least 25cm (10in) long.

METHOD

1. Separate and discard one candle.
2. Hang the remaining pair over the hook and tie on the wick of the third candle, so that the tops of all three candles are at the same level.
3. Plait the candles together.
4. Squeeze the bottom ends together smoothly, and flatten the base so that the candle can stand up. Hang it up and allow it to cool for one hour.

The candle that was discarded from the plaiting process can be finished in a different way – by twisting. However, first of all, its diameter must be increased by further dipping.

Plaiting the candles.

Squeezing the bottom ends of the candles together.

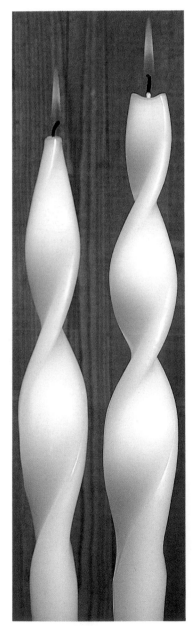

Twisted candles.

How to – twisted candles

EQUIPMENT AND MATERIALS

Rolling-pin and flat rolling surface; knife; one freshly dipped candle 25cm (10in) long and 2.5cm (1in) in diameter.

METHOD

1. Roll out the upper part of the candle until it is about 6mm (¼in) thick. Leave the bottom 2.5cm (1in) unrolled so that it can fit into a candle holder. If the candle cracks whilst rolling, then it has become too hard. Soften it by dipping it for three seconds at 71°C (160°F) and then waiting for thirty seconds.
2. Hold the candle upside-down, with the unrolled base in one hand and the flattened part nearest the base between the thumb and forefinger of your other hand.

3. Pull the candle slowly upwards, sliding it between your thumb and forefinger and turning it steadily.
4. Repeat the process to give a more exaggerated twist.
5. Trim the base flat and allow the candle to cool for one hour.

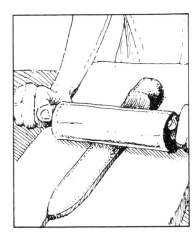

Flattening the candle.

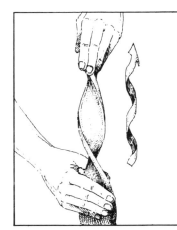

Twisting the candle.

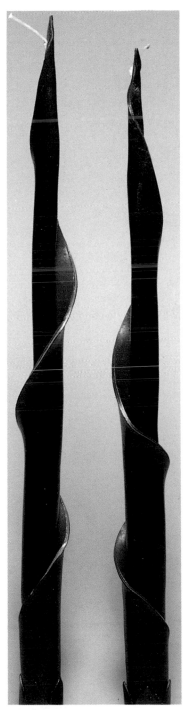

Flared spiral candles in pink and black.

Rolling

Simple candles can be made by rolling a sheet of wax around a prepared wick. The method of making a wax sheet that follows is particularly useful and should spark off many new ideas. It uses a large quantity of wax because of the height of the candles, but you can experiment with lesser quantities by using a smaller plywood template.

If, at any stage, the wax becomes too cold to work easily, then you can warm it gently with a hair dryer.

How to – flared spiral candles

EQUIPMENT AND MATERIALS
Double boiler; thermometer; triangular template (piece of plywood with sanded edges) 27 × 10 × 29cm (10¾ × 4 × 11½ in) with wire attached to one corner to hold whilst dipping; two tall dipping cans; bowl of water; 10kg (22lb) dip and carve wax (paraffin wax will do if necessary); 100g (approx. 5 discs) pink dye; 30g (approx. 1½ discs) chalky white dye; 200g (approx. 10 discs) black dye; two 30cm (12in) lengths of 1.25cm (½in) wick.

METHOD
1. Soak the plywood template in water for thirty minutes.
2. Heat 5kg (11lb) of wax to 71°C (160°F), prime the wicks, then add the pink and chalky white dyes.

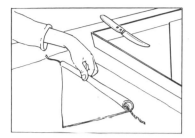

Rolling the wax into a tube.

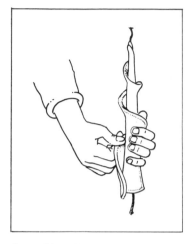

Smoothing the exposed edge into a spiral fin.

3. Heat the other 5kg (11lb) of wax to the same temperature and add the black dye. (To get the dyes to disperse fully, it may be necessary to heat the wax to a higher temperature, and then allow it to cool for dipping.)
4. Remove the template from the water and shake off any excess drops.
5. Dip the template in the pink wax and wait for one minute. Repeat this five times more. Then, do the same with the black wax.
6. Wait until the wax is rubbery, then peel the wax from each face of the template.
7. Place one of the wax triangles pink side up and turn back the longest edge.
8. Lay the wick along the longest side, about 1.25cm (½in) from the edge.
9. Fold the edge of the wax over the wick, and then roll it into a tube. Turn up the exposed edge with your fingers and smooth it into a spiral fin.
10. Flatten the base against your work surface and allow the candle to cool. Repeat with the other half of the wax.

Beeswax sheets

With one particular variety of wax, the technique of rolling really comes into its own. Beeswax is available in preformed honeycomb sheets, usually 34 × 20cm (13½ × 8in) in size. The sheets come in a variety of natural colours, ranging from creamy white to a rich medium brown, and dyed red and green. Beeswax sheets are workable at normal room temperature, although in cold weather they may need to be held near a heater for a few minutes until they soften.

Rolled beeswax candles can be very simple, or quite complicated – the choice is entirely yours. Candles can be straight or tapered, and sheets of contrasting natural shades can be rolled together for added effect. The sheets may also be cut into strips, which can be woven or wrapped around the outside of the candle.

How to – tapered beeswax candles

EQUIPMENT AND MATERIALS
Knife; metre (yard) rule; scissors; beeswax sheet 34 × 20cm (13½ × 8in); two 28cm (11in) lengths of 1.25cm (½in) wick.

METHOD
1. Cut the sheet in two across the diagonal.
2. Take one of the pieces and lay a wick along the shortest side of the triangle. The extra length of wick should project beyond the point.

3. Fold the edge of the sheet over the wick and roll the candle. Take care to produce a flat base.

4. Secure the loose end of the sheet by pressing it into the side of the candle.

5. Trim the wick to about 1.25cm (½ in). Pinch a small piece of wax from the under-side of the base and squeeze it into the projecting wick. This ensures that the candle is ready to light.

6. Repeat the process with the other piece of beeswax sheet, but lay it the other way round. The finished candles will then be mirror images of each other.

A selection of candles made from beeswax sheets.

Hand modelling

Wax is a very versatile material, and there is no limit to what creativity and imagination can achieve. With just a little skill and preparation, an ordinary dipped candle can be transformed into a realistic piece of wax sculpture – and a really exciting candle.

The instructions in this section are a little more complicated than the ones that you have been following until now, so read each sequence through carefully before you begin. If there is anything that you are not sure of, then refer back to the previous pages.

Floating rose candles.

Perfumed wax flowers

Scented candles are a colourful and effective alternative to 'room deodorants', and they can also be used to provide that extra touch of atmosphere. By modelling flowers from scented wax, you can make a stunning perfumed centre-piece for a special dinner-table.

How to – floating roses

EQUIPMENT AND MATERIALS

Double boiler; thermometer; grease-proof paper; smooth-edged pastry cutter, or palette knife; wax glue; 1kg (2lb 3oz) dip and carve wax; eight 5cm (2in) lengths of 1.25cm (½in) wick; rose-scented wax perfume; wax pigment. These materials are sufficient to make eight floating rose candles.

METHOD

1. Melt the wax, heat it to 71°C (160°F), and prime the wicks.
2. Lay out some sheets of grease-proof paper. Switch off the heat, and add twelve drops of perfume to the wax.
3. Carefully pour out the wax on to the paper so that it forms layers about 3mm (⅛in) thick, and allow it to cool until it is rubbery.
4. Cut petal shapes with the pastry cutter or palette knife. You will need petals of different sizes. Curve them with your fingers.
5. Squeeze two small petals around a wick and build up a rose flower by gluing on larger petals. Work quickly and make only one or two flowers at once. Wax that has cooled too much and become brittle can be softened with a hair dryer.
6. When your roses have cooled down completely, they can be painted with wax pigment.

All candles will float, but these ones will float upright. Placed in clear glass bowls and lit, they make a novel alternative to traditional forms of candle-light.

Wax fungi

Fly agaric is one of the many fungi found in fields and hedgerows. Incidentally, it is extremely poisonous, so do not be tempted to eat the real thing. Other fungi have equally distinctive shapes and colouring, and by modifying the basic technique described on page 28 a whole botanical garden of colourful fungi can be created.

A colourful collection of fungi candles.

Bending the candle.

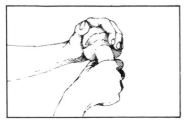

Smoothing the cap.

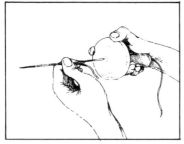

Re-threading the wick.

Dipping the whole candle.

Dipping the cap in red wax.

How to – fly agaric toadstool

EQUIPMENT AND MATERIALS

Double boiler; thermometer; dipping can; wicking needle; one 25cm (10in) freshly made dipped candle about 2.5cm (1in) in diameter; paraffin wax initially at 71°C (160°F) – the quantity will depend upon the size of your dipping can; 250g (9oz) bright red overdipping wax; egg-cupful of undyed overdipping wax.

METHOD

1. Hold the candle in one hand, and with the other pull the wick straight out of the end of the candle. Put it aside for later use.
2. Bend the candle just below the midpoint, and wrap the upper part around to form the basis for the toadstool's cap. Shape the stalk, flaring it slightly at the base.
3. Hold the stalk and turn the cap against the palm of your hand to form a smooth rounded shape. To keep it soft, frequently re-dip the candle into the paraffin wax. Allow it to cool for thirty seconds after each dip.
4. Use the wicking needle to re-thread the wick up through the stalk. Tie a knot in the wick at the stalk end, then pull the wick up so that the knot embeds in the base. Do not trim the other end of the wick.
5. Heat the paraffin wax to 82°C (180°F), then re-dip the entire candle, stalk end first. Two three-second dips, separated by a one minute cooling period, will give an overall smooth appearance. Flatten the base so that the toadstool stands up, and allow it to cool for thirty minutes.
6. Heat the red overdipping wax to 82°C (180°F) and dip the upper side of the cap into it for three seconds. After thirty seconds, dip it again for another three seconds.
7. Dip the sharp end of the wicking needle into the undyed overdipping wax at 82°C (180°F) and hold it there for about fifteen seconds. Then, place the point on the toadstool's cap, allowing the wax to run off and form a raised white dot. Repeat this to give a natural appearance, then allow the candle to cool fully for one hour.

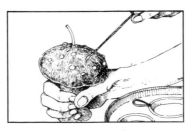

Forming the white spots.

MOULDED CANDLES

Moulded candles

Most candles are made in moulds. This technique makes full use of the ease with which wax turns from solid to liquid and back again. However, moulded does not mean machine-made. Moulded candles are every bit as handmade as those produced by dipping, and they provide endless scope for exciting variations, from vivid pop art colours to subtle impressionist landscapes.

Candle moulds are available in a bewildering variety of shapes and sizes, but in all cases the basic technique is the same. A prepared wick is threaded through the mould, which is then filled with molten wax. The mould is cooled in a water bath and is periodically topped up with wax. When cold, the candle is removed and the wick is trimmed.

It sounds simple, and it is. However, I do urge you to read through the following three pages carefully, even if you have no intention of making a one-colour candle. Some of the candles in this section can take several hours to produce, and, because 'there's many a slip twixt cup and lip', a little patience and

A selection of moulds used for candlemaking.

practice now might well save you heartache at the end of some future afternoon.

Moulds

All the candles in this section are based on easily available commercial moulds. However, for the more adventurous, there are some notes on page 46 on improvising and making your own moulds. The basic types of mould are listed here.

Rigid plastic Usually transparent, these are ideal for the beginner and are available in a variety of geometric shapes.

Glass These moulds produce candles with a high gloss finish, but they are fragile and limited to cylindrical shapes.

Metal These are sturdy and have excellent cooling properties.

Flexible PVC These are ideal for irregular shapes, such as candle fruits, and give a good finish.

Rubber These moulds produce candles with a matt finish. They tend to deteriorate with repeated use, but are ideal for high relief surfaces.

Most moulded candles start with a primed wick. If you have forgotten how to dip your wick, then go back to page 15 and refresh your memory.

How to – wicking up

EQUIPMENT AND MATERIALS
Cylindrical mould; wicking needle; bowl of water; mould seal; one primed wick.

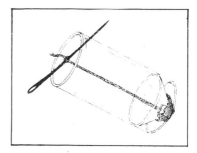
Wicking up the mould.

METHOD
1. Thread the primed wick up through the small hole in the end of the mould. The coated end should always be at the 'burning end' of the candle.
2. Place the wicking needle across the base of the mould and tie the wick to it.
3. Pull the other end of the wick tight and secure it with a lump of mould seal – this is reusable so do not be stingy.
4. Hold the sealed end of the mould under water to check that the mould seal is watertight.

Water baths

Wax poured into a mould takes a long time to cool. The cooling time can be shortened by using a water bath, that is, a bowl of cold water. Candles can be allowed to cool at room temperature, but water cooling improves appearance and gives smoother mould release.

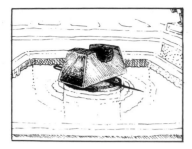

Weighting the mould in the water bath.

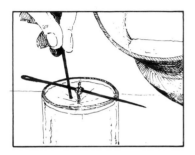

Topping up the mould with hot wax.

Almost any large bowl can be used, provided that its base is level enough for the mould to stand upright and it is deep enough for the mould. Normally, a water bath is filled to within 1.25cm (½in) of the base of the inverted mould. An ideal temperature for water baths is 10–15°C (50–59°F); below 10°C (50°F) thermal shock may cause cracking. In midwinter it may be necessary to warm up water from the cold tap.

Wax floats, and so will a filled mould. Therefore, a weight (1kg/2lb) must be used to keep the mould stable. The technique of positioning the weight is worth practising, as toppling a freshly poured candle is not the right way to find out that your weight does not balance properly.

Topping up

As wax cools it shrinks, and this shrinkage is what enables a candle to be removed from its mould. However, not all of the shrinkage is desirable, and the candle must be topped up carefully as it cools.

The cooling wax forms a well around the wick area. This must be filled, but not overfilled, and it is very important that no hot wax spills over between the candle and the mould. If this occurs, then the candle will become very difficult to remove from the mould.

Successful topping up depends upon a steady hand and precise control over the amount of wax that you are delivering. It also helps to use a can or pan with a suitable spout, that is, one that is not too wide. To begin with, you may find it helpful to practise pouring small amounts of water into a narrow-necked bottle.

The secrets of a good moulded candle are correct pouring temperatures and knowing how to play the waiting game. Use the cooling time to good purpose, and do not let the clock oppress you. Whatever you do, if you want good results then learn to resist temptation. Do not fiddle or poke at the well until the first hour has passed, and once you have topped up the candle leave it alone – a watched candle never sets!

Waxes for moulding

Never make assumptions about waxes and moulds; always check the instructions thoroughly. With most rigid moulds, a quantity (usually 10 per cent) of stearin can be added to paraffin wax to increase the amount of shrinkage. But with some other moulds, such as rubber, the stearin rots the surface of the mould and must not be used.

Beeswax presents problems when used in moulds because it is so sticky. With rigid moulds, a release agent must always be applied to the inside of the mould if more than 10 per cent beeswax is to be used.

One-colour candles

These are the simplest moulded candles and will provide you with valuable experience. All of the basic moulding techniques are employed, and once you have made one you can move on with confidence to more sophisticated candles.

The instructions are based on one of the most common types of commercial mould. If you use a different mould and are not sure about the quantity of wax, then fill the mould with water and measure it. Every 100cm³ (⅕pt) of water represents 90g (3¼ oz) of cold wax.

Melting the stearin.

How to – one-colour candle

EQUIPMENT AND MATERIALS

Double boiler; saucepan; thermometer; cylindrical mould 20cm (8in) tall and 5cm (2in) in diameter; wicking needle; water bath; weight; scissors; 225g (8oz) paraffin wax; 25g (1oz) stearin; 2.5g (approx. ⅛ disc) red wax dye; 25cm (10in) length of 5cm (2in) wick; mould seal.

Adding the paraffin wax.

METHOD

1. Melt the stearin in the double boiler, and then add the dye.
2. When the dye has dissolved, add the paraffin wax.
3. Whilst the wax is melting, wick up the mould (see page 31). Check that the mould seal is watertight. If it leaks, then dry the inside of the mould thoroughly before wicking up again.
4. Heat the wax to 93°C (199°F) and carefully pour it into the middle of the inverted mould, trying not to touch the sides. Do not fill the mould completely, but leave about 1.25cm (½ in) at the end.

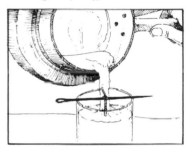

Pouring the wax into the inverted mould.

5. Wait two minutes, then give the mould a sharp tap with the scissors or a spoon handle. This will shake loose any bubbles of air that are attached to the inside of the mould.
6. Stand the mould in the water bath using the weight to hold it down (see opposite). The level of the water in the bath should be the same as the level of the wax in the mould. Allow it to cool for one hour.
7. A conical well will form around the wick. Remove the mould from the bath and prick the surface of the well with a wicking needle.

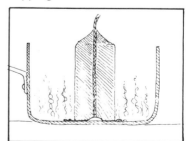

Tapping the mould.

8. Re-heat the wax to 93°C (199°F) and carefully top up the well (see opposite). Do not top up beyond the original level, as this will overfill the mould and make the candle difficult to extract.
9. Replace the mould in the water bath for a further hour until the candle has cooled down completely.
10. Take the mould out of the water and remove the mould seal. Turn the mould the right way up and your candle will slide out. With the scissors, trim the wick flush with the base, then use a warm pan to level the base so that the candle stands upright.

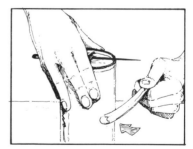

Levelling the base of the candle.

Page 34: *a selection of one-colour candles.*
Page 35: *a selection of layered and angled layered candles.*

Multicoloured candles

Different coloured waxes can be used in the same candle to great effect. Bright, primary colours can be paired in eye-catching contrast. Alternatively, subtle, toning shades can produce a restful and evocative result. The choice is all yours.

Once you have mastered the techniques outlined on the following pages, there is no end to the potential for experiment. With practice, you will be able to transform a vision seen in the mind's eye into the physical reality of a beautiful candle.

Layered candles

Pouring alternate layers of contrasting wax produces a two-tone, banded candle. The layers can be as thick or as thin as you like, although layers less than 1.25cm (½ in) thick are difficult to pour.

Another idea is to use just one colour, but start with a very pale shade and then add a little more dye each time you pour. The graduated tones of the finished candle will blend imperceptibly into each other.

The candle described below has layers at angles for added interest. I have used a conical mould because the sloped sides enhance the effect of the angles.

How to – angled layered candle

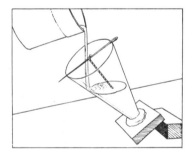

Pouring wax into the tilting mould.

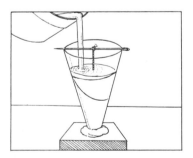

Pouring wax into the upright mould.

EQUIPMENT AND MATERIALS
Double boiler; thermometer; conical mould 12.5cm (5in) high; tilting block; wicking needle; water bath; weight; scissors; paper tissue; 165g (6oz) paraffin wax; 15g (½ oz) stearin; red, green and yellow dyes; 17.5cm (7in) length of 2.5cm (1in) wick; mould seal.

METHOD
1. Wick up the mould (see page 31).
2. Melt 55g (2oz) paraffin wax and 5g (⅙ oz) stearin and add yellow dye. You will need a strong colour so use plenty of dye. Heat the wax to 93°C (199°F).
3. Place the mould on the tilting block and pour in the yellow wax. After one minute, tap the mould to release any air bubbles. Allow it to cool until the surface is rubbery and will break, not bend, when prodded.
4. Wipe out the double boiler with tissue and, using the same quantities, prepare the green wax and heat it to 82°C (180°F).
5. Tilt the mould to the other side and pour in the green wax. Tap out any air and allow it to cool until the surface is rubbery.
6. Prepare the red wax and pour it into the upright mould at 82°C (180°F), making a level base. Tap out any air and then place it in the water bath to cool for half an hour. If necessary, then top up with red wax at 93°C (199°F).
7. Allow the candle to cool for a further hour, then remove it from the mould, trim the wick, and flatten the base.

Landscapes in wax

By combining the layering technique with a little simple sculpture, you can create a candle that contains a miniature landscape of a river, hills and mountains.

This candle involves five or six different colours, and you will probably find it easier to melt and mix all the separate colours beforehand. The best results are achieved with quite subtle colours, and wax only shows its true colour when cold. Mixing the colours beforehand allows you to judge and adjust them before you start pouring. The proportions of colour in this candle are approximately as follows: sky blue 40 per cent; pale green 10 per cent; mid-green 25 per cent; dark green 15 per cent; dark blue 10 per cent (or dark blue 5 per cent and brown 5 per cent).

Landscape candle.

How to – landscape candle

EQUIPMENT AND MATERIALS

Double boiler; thermometer; cylindrical mould 20cm (8in) tall and 5cm (2in) in diameter; wicking needle; teaspoon with rounded handle; matchstick; water bath; weight; scissors; 225g (8oz) paraffin wax; 25g (1oz) stearin; blue, green, and brown (if required) dyes; 25cm (10in) length of 5cm (2in) wick; mould seal.

METHOD

1. Wick up the mould. Melt the paraffin wax and stearin, and mix up all of the colours in the proportions given above.
2. Heat the pale blue wax to 82°C (180°F) and pour it into the mould. Wait for one minute and tap out any air. Place it in the water bath to cool until the wax is set but still warm.
3. Remove it from the water and, using the teaspoon handle, carve out some pointed mountain peaks.
4. Heat the pale green wax to 82°C (180°F) and pour it into the mould. Tap out any air and allow it to cool until the wax is set but still warm.
5. Use the spoon to carve out the hills below the peaks. Heat the mid-green wax and pour it in. Allow it to set.
6. Now carve out some foothills, trying to make them overlap the hills. Pour in the dark green wax and allow it to cool.
7. With the matchstick, trace the course of the river down one of the overlapping valleys. The river should widen towards the base and make a lake. Pour in the dark blue wax to fill the river and lake. Allow it to cool.
8. The final thin layer can be either brown for soil, or more blue to create an island landscape.
9. After pouring all the layers, allow the finished candle to cool in the water bath for a further hour before removing it from the mould. Finally, trim the wick and flatten the base of the candle.

Detail of landscape candle.

Swirling and chunks

Bright, cheerful candles can be made by pouring coloured wax over chunks of contrasting wax. This is a good way of using up 'failed' candles or any other odd bits of wax.

Star-shaped moulds are the best for chunk-laden candles because they provide the most opportunities to place chunks to good effect. Otherwise, the procedure is the same as for a one-colour candle (see page 33).

An exciting refinement is to pour in plain wax and then spoon in dye so that it creates swirling patterns as it spreads. Doing this means using wax that is hotter than the boiling point of water, so the wax must be heated directly. Please be careful when doing this, as at these temperatures wax becomes flammable. Timing and temperature are critical with this type of candle. The wax must be hot but the dyes should only be warm. The secret is in putting the candle into the water bath before the swirls of colour lose definition.

How to – swirly chunked candle

EQUIPMENT AND MATERIALS

Saucepan; egg poacher; thermometer; wicking needle; three teaspoons; water bath; weight; 60g (2oz) coloured wax poured out into a sheet about 7mm (¼in) thick and allowed to go cold; 90g (3¼oz) paraffin wax; 10g (⅓oz) stearin; three pieces of dye in contrasting colours; star-shaped mould 15cm (6in) high; 20cm (8in) length of 2.5cm (1in) wick; mould seal.

METHOD

1. Wick up the mould. Break up the sheet of wax into 1–2cm (½–¾in) chunks and place them in the mould. Take care not to disturb or dislodge the wick.
2. Melt the dyes in the egg poacher – they should only just be liquid.
3. Melt the wax and stearin in the saucepan and heat to 127°C (260°F). Gently pour it into the centre of the mould, covering all of the chunks.
4. Using a different spoon for each colour, spoon drops of dye into the mould. Allow about forty-five seconds for the dyes to swirl, then place the mould in a cold water bath and weight it. Allow it to cool for two hours.
5. Release your candle by gently pressing the sides of the mould outwards whilst supporting the points with your fingers.

Opposite: a swirly chunked candle.

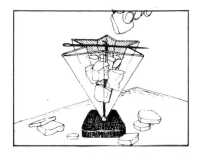

Placing wax chunks in the mould.

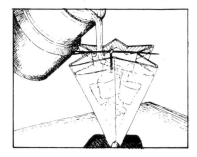

Pouring wax/stearin mixture into the mould.

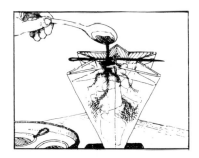

Spooning drops of melted dye into the mould.

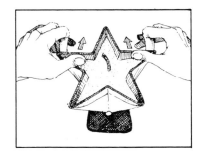

Releasing the candle.

Candle fruits

These look good enough to eat and certainly too good to burn. A well-made candle fruit is virtually indistinguishable from the real thing and makes a wonderful novelty present. The illusion of reality can be enhanced even further by the use of the appropriate fruit perfume. In a bowl, candle fruits make an appetizing display that will not discolour or go mouldy. Individual fruits can be incorporated into seasonal flower arrangements, or simply placed on a shelf for a touch of colour and something to tease the eye.

Above: a colourful stall of tempting candle fruits.

Opposite: a selection of chunked candles.

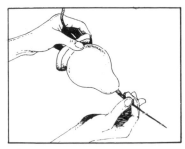

Threading the unprimed wick.

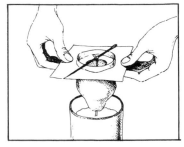

Lowering the mould into the water bath.

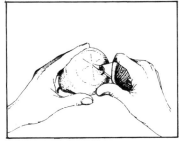

Peeling the mould back on itself.

Trimming the base of the candle.

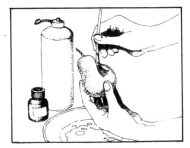

Painting the candle.

Wicks and water baths

Candle fruits are made in flexible moulds, and there are two essential points to remember when using this type of mould. Firstly, you do not prime the wick beforehand. Doing so just increases the possibility of molten wax leaking out of the mould. When new, flexible moulds have no hole at the upper end, so you must make the hole with the wicking needle. Make it as small as you possibly can. Secondly, a suitable water bath needs to be selected for each mould. Large quantities of water will cause the mould to distort as it cools. For the best results, there should be no more than 5cm (2in) of water between the mould and the sides of the water bath.

How to – candle pear

EQUIPMENT AND MATERIALS

Double boiler; thermometer; flexible rubber pear mould; wicking needle; water bath only slightly larger than the mould; stiff cardboard template to support neck of mould; cloth; paintbrush; craft knife; dipping can; washing-up liquid; white spirit; 240g (8½ oz) paraffin wax; 3g (⅐ disc) 'pear fruit' dye; 15cm (6in) length of 3.75cm (1½in) wick; burnt sienna poster paint; sufficient green or yellow wax (not too strong a colour) to dip the finished candle.

METHOD

1. Melt the wax in the double boiler and stir in the 'pear fruit' dye.
2. Use the wicking needle to thread the unprimed wick up through the mould. Rest the needle across the base of the mould and tie the wick to it. Gently pull the wick tight.
3. Fit the template around the neck of the mould, and then stand the mould in the empty dipping can.
4. Heat the wax to 93°C (199°F) and pour it into the mould, covering the top of the neck. Wait for one minute.
5. Carefully lift the mould up by the template and tap it with a finger to release any air bubbles. Lower the mould into the water bath.
6. As soon as the surface of the wax at the neck starts to solidify, prick it with the wicking needle. You must keep breaking this surface throughout the cooling process.
7. After ten minutes, change the water in the bath. Do this again after a further ten minutes, and again ten minutes later.
8. Allow the mould to continue cooling for another hour and a half. Break the surface at the neck every fifteen minutes or so.
9. Reheat the wax to 93°C (199°F) and top up the mould. Lift the mould out of the water and allow it to cool for one hour.
10. Remove the template. Pick off any lumps of wax that have leaked out of the top. Cover the outside of the mould with

washing-up liquid, then peel the mould back on itself to remove the candle.

11. Carefully trim the base of the candle to a rounded shape.

12. Mix some burnt sienna poster paint with a little water and add a drop of washing-up liquid. Brush the mixture over the whole surface of the candle and allow it to dry. Wipe off any excess colour with a cloth dampened with white spirit.

13. For the final realistic shine, dip the finished candle in green or yellow wax heated to 82°C (180°F) for four seconds. Wait for one minute, then re-dip for two seconds. After ten minutes, polish your pear with a wet tissue.

Candle fruits can provide an unusual focal point for a supper table.

Pour-in pour-out candles

This technique is exactly the opposite of overdipping (see pages 18–19). By pouring in and pouring out, layers of wax are built up on the inside of a mould. It is possible to have as many layers as you like, but I have found that good results can be obtained with just two. When preparing wax for this type of candle, remember that the second pour (the underlayer) must be strongly dyed if the colour is to show through. Four times the normal amount of dye will give you colours of sufficient strength.

Any type of mould can be used. Flexible moulds give especially interesting results, because the overlayer tends to be thicker in some places than others. This creates attractive variations in the colour show-through. For beginners, I recommend a star mould because its shape permits the wax to cool quickly and the process can be watched.

The amount of time needed for the first layer to form can be as little as one minute or as long as twenty minutes, depending upon the cooling rate of the mould. As a guide, the overlayer should be about 3mm (⅛ in) thick.

How to – pour-in pour-out candle

EQUIPMENT AND MATERIALS
As for an ordinary moulded candle (see page 33), but with enough wax to fill the mould twice (once with each colour). If you are using a flexible mould, then you will need a stand to hold the mould upright.

METHOD
1. Wick up the mould and fill it with wax at 82°C (180°F). Wait for a 3mm (⅛ in) layer to set.
2. Pour off all the wax that has not solidified and wait for a few minutes.
3. Fill the mould with wax of the second colour at 82°C (180°F) and allow it to cool.
4. After two hours, prick the well and top up with wax at 82°C (180°F). Allow the candle to cool for a further two hours before removing it from the mould.

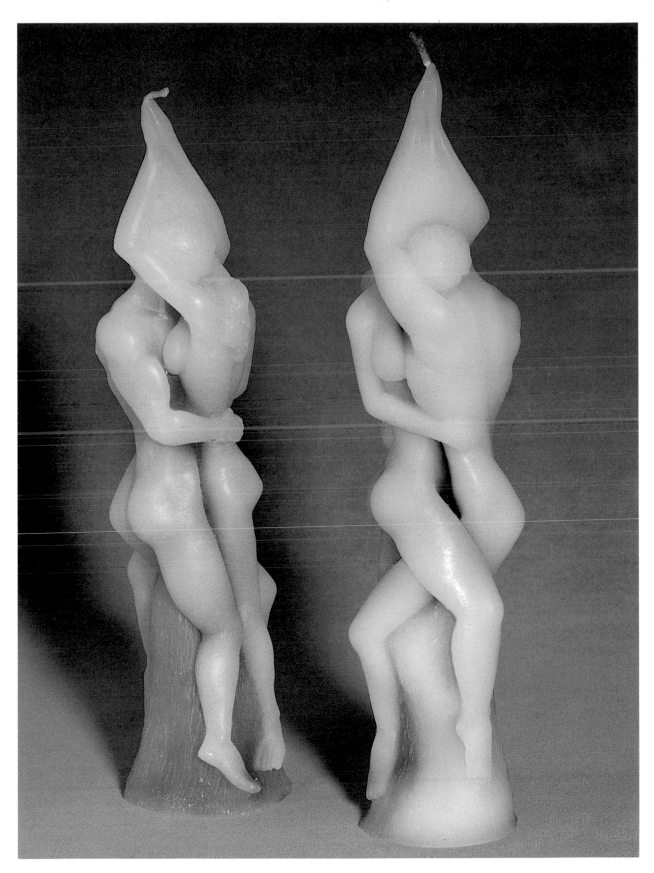

Making your own moulds

Simple moulds can be improvised from household packaging, such as yoghurt pots and toothpaste pumps, but please take care as hot wax can be very messy. Here is a simple 'rule of thumb' – if it will hold boiling water without collapsing, then you can use it as a candle mould, always remembering, of course, that you have to be able to remove your candle after it has cooled. Shapes that are larger at the top than they are at the base cannot be used. Think about it!

Corrugated cardboard makes excellent candles. The only real problem is finding a way to shape and seal the 'top' end and stabilize the wick. For a conical top, the end of a washing-up liquid bottle can be taped to the end. For a flat-topped candle, you will need to cut a circle of thin plastic and make a hole in the centre with a wicking needle.

Spherical moulds can be made from old tennis balls. Cut the ball into two halves. In the centre of one half, make a hole about 3cm (1¼ in) in diameter through which to pour the wax. In the centre of the other half, make a tiny hole for the wick. Tape the two halves together and wick up the mould as normal.

Once you have gained confidence, you may wish to try making your own moulds from instant moulding compounds. A number of these are available from good craft shops, and, whilst you should follow the instructions provided exactly, the basic principle is the same. The object to be moulded is coated with release agent, and is then covered with a layer (or several) of moulding compound. The compound is allowed to set (usually for about one hour), and then the mould is gently peeled off. Depending upon the type of compound used, it should then be treated as a PVC or rubber mould (see page 42).

Mastery of this technique opens up enormous possibilities – candle sculptures, candle china dogs, candle busts of great composers, candle wine bottles, even candles of your own (or a friend's) hand or foot!

SURFACE
TECHNIQUES

Surface techniques

Casting a candle is only half the story. In many respects, a freshly cast candle is just the raw material for the candle-finisher's craft. In this section, I describe a number of basic techniques for enhancing and embellishing the appearance of a candle. In the following section, I take this a stage further. With some candles, making the candle and finishing it are part and parcel of the same creative process.

Pressed flowers and grasses

These should be prepared at least one week before you intend to use them. Wild grasses can be used, but if you are going to use flowers then please buy cultivated flowers from a stall or shop. Do not pick wild flowers.

How to – pressed flower candle

EQUIPMENT AND MATERIALS
Electric iron; three teaspoons; cloth; thermometer; dipping can containing sufficient undyed paraffin wax to cover the candle; pressed flowers; candle to be decorated.

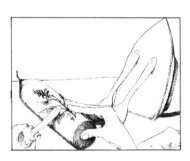

Attaching a pressed flower to the candle.

METHOD
1. Set the iron on a medium heat and rest the teaspoons against it to heat them up.
2. Take one of the flowers and position it on the surface of the candle.
3. Take one of the spoons and press it all over the flower, melting it into the wax. Hold the spoon in a cloth to prevent burning your fingers.
4. Repeat with the other flowers in the arrangement, changing spoons as they cool down.
5. Heat the wax in the can to 96°C (205°F) and dip the candle for three seconds. Press down any petals or leaves that are sticking out and dip again for two seconds. At first the wax will be opaque, but it will clear as it cools. Stand the candle on its base and leave it for half an hour before handling.

Opposite: a selection of pressed flower candles.

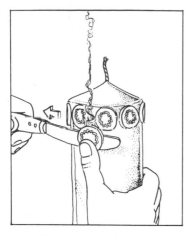

Attaching chunks of coloured wax to the candle.

Appliqué

With this technique, chunks of coloured wax are stuck on to the outside of a white candle. As the candle burns down, the flame illuminates the chunks from the inside, and they glow as if the candle was studded with uncut gems.

Appliqué works best with chunks that are strongly coloured but are still translucent. If too much dye has been used, then the chunks will be opaque.

The process is very simple. All you need is a bowl of water at 96°C (205°F) and a round-ended kitchen knife. Heat the blade in the water, dry it on a kitchen towel, then press the flat of the blade against the candle, holding a chunk of wax against the other side. Slide the blade from between them, and the chunk will stick to the candle. Alternatively, use wax glue. After you have covered the candle, you can dip it in undyed wax as for the pressed flower candle (see page 48).

With practice, you can create designs or even pictures with appliqué chunks. As your candle burns down, it will reveal a 'stained glass window' of coloured wax.

Right: a detail of an appliquéd candle.
Far right: a selection of appliquéd candles.

50

Cutting the coloured candle into slices.

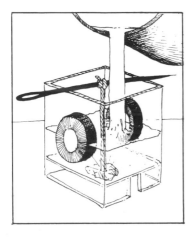

Pouring the wax/stearin mixture into the prepared mould.

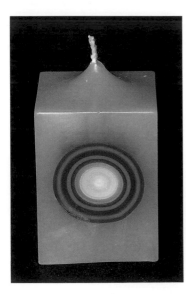

Bull's-eye candle.

Inlays

This is not strictly a finishing technique, but I have included it here because it is a surface effect. Basically, pieces of contrasting wax are stuck to the inside of a mould before it is filled. When the mould is removed, the wax pieces are revealed as inlays in the surface of the candle. The bull's-eye candle is an attractive design, with a slightly spooky effect when lit that children seem to love.

How to – bull's-eye candle

EQUIPMENT AND MATERIALS
Double boiler; thermometer; three dipping cans; mould 12.5cm (5in) square; wicking needle; water bath; weight; sharp knife; electric iron or white spirit; mould seal; one coloured dipped candle 2cm (¾ in) in diameter; dyed wax in three different colours for overdipping; 150g (5oz) paraffin wax; 15g (½ oz) stearin; 17cm (6¾ in) length of 3.75cm (1½ in) wick; wax glue.

METHOD
1. Overdip three additional colours on to the candle (see pages 18–19). Three three-second dips in each colour should be sufficient. The final diameter should be approximately 3.5cm (1½ in).
2. Allow the candle to cool, then cut two 2.5cm (1in) slices. With a drop of wax glue, stick these in the centre of opposite faces of the mould. Wick up the mould as normal.
3. Heat the paraffin wax and stearin to 82°C (180°F) and pour it into the mould. Tap out the air and place the mould in the water bath.
4. After forty minutes, prick the well and top up with wax at 93°C (199°F). Allow it to cool completely.
5. After removal from the mould, the sides of the candle can be smoothed against a warm electric iron, or polished with white spirit and buffed with a wet tissue.

Carving

Wax is extremely easy to carve, and you can practise on any old candle or lump of wax. As to what to carve with, use whatever gives the best results – craft knives, penknives, ends of spoons. You can even buy sets of wax carving tools, but you are unlikely to need these unless you are planning a series of family portraits in candles.

The secret is to remove only small pieces of wax at a time. Remember that once you have carved it off, you cannot stick it back, so plan your carving carefully. When your design is completed, burnish the carved surfaces with a rounded teaspoon handle.

With this variation on a one-colour candle (see page 33), you can combine carving with colour.

METHOD

1. Wick up the mould and pour in undyed wax. Allow it to cool until a layer about 5mm (¼ in) thick has solidified on the sides.
2. Pour the liquid wax back into the pan, dye it strongly and heat it to 88°C (190°F). Pour the coloured wax into the mould, then cool and top up as normal.
3. When the candle is completely cold, a design can be carved through the plain wax to reveal the colour beneath.

Carved candle.

53

Dip and iron back

The electric iron was a great invention for candlemakers. It is a handy tool which provides a smooth heated surface that is superb for removing wax to a uniform level. Candles with a high relief surface can be overdipped in a contrasting colour, which is then ironed away from the high points of the design to reveal the colour beneath.

With very high relief surfaces, more than one colour can be overdipped. It is best to overdip darker colours before lighter ones.

A selection of candles made by the dip and iron back method.

METHOD

1. Each coloured layer needs at least three dips of three seconds each, with one minute between dips.

2. After each colour layer, the candle should be cooled in cold water for five minutes, then dried thoroughly before dipping in the next colour.

3. The iron should be set on a medium heat, and you should work over a tray or sheet of newspaper to catch the drips of wax. Apply the candle to the iron, not the iron to the candle.

Overdipping the candle.

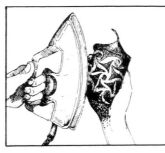

Ironing the candle.

Hammering

Wax is a soft material and care has to be taken against accidental knocks which leave unsightly dents in a candle. This ability of wax to receive an impression when struck can be exploited to excellent decorative effect by hammering.

One of my favourite finishes is that obtained by using a ball-peen hammer. This works especially well on round candles, but care has to be taken to get the spacing equal.

Place the candle comfortably in your lap and lay the ball of the hammer against it. Give the hammer a sharp tap with a mallet or block of wood, not with a metal object. The ball will leave a

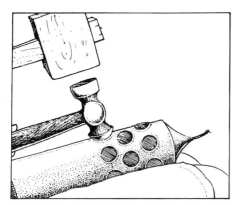

Hammering the candle.

smooth rounded impression. Repeat the process to build up an overall pattern.

Objects other than a ball-peen hammer can be used to make impressions, but they should be rounded to avoid breaking up the surface. Old bath taps, brass buttons, and various bits of kitchen equipment can all be used to good effect.

Painting

Wax is the best medium for painting on wax. You can use acrylic paint, but I do not recommend it because it can interfere with the smooth burning of the candle.

Any type of wax will do, but beeswax is best, and it can be coloured any shade you choose. It is important to colour the wax with candle pigment because dyes tend to migrate. The wax must be kept warm whilst you paint and an egg poacher is ideal for this. Use an ordinary artist's paintbrush and work with swift smooth strokes, one stroke at a time. The wax cools quickly, so you will need to re-dip the brush frequently. When re-dipping, leave the brush in the wax for at least twenty seconds, so that any wax that has solidified on the brush is completely melted. For speed, use two brushes alternately.

Once you have painted wax on to a candle it can be difficult to remove. You can allow the wax to cool and then rub it off with white spirit, but this will probably mar the surface of the candle. To avoid this, practise your design on a sheet of glass or mirror. Afterwards, the wax can be removed easily with hot water.

Painting the candle.

ADVANCED SURFACE TECHNIQUES

Advanced surface techniques

This section is concerned with extending your control over the final appearance of your candle. It also provides me with the opportunity to introduce you to the work of two contemporary candlemakers whose work I greatly admire. Some of their candles go beyond being merely decorative candles; they are beautiful objects, pure and simple, and should probably be termed sculpture.

None of the techniques outlined here is very complicated. If you have worked steadily through this book, then you should have no difficulty in following the instructions and producing some stunning candles. There are only two limiting factors – your creative ability and your patience.

Creative candlemaking requires a special type of patience, one which is alert and active – in other words, watch carefully what is going on. You may find it useful to make notes whilst you work, for example, recording how long the cooling period was at a particular stage or how hot the wax was during dipping. Keeping a record of this sort will enable you to check up on failed candles and pin-point the cause of any problems.

Dip and carve

This technique is so simple that you already know how to do it, as all the elements are covered in previous sections. However, it is such a versatile technique that it deserves further consideration.

The first candle that I describe is one of my own, and it is so easy that it hardly needs any explanation. I have included it for two reasons; firstly, because this method produces extremely attractive candles, and, secondly, because it is deeply satisfying to make. Slowly carving back through layers of coloured wax is one of the most pleasurable experiences I know. The main ingredient necessary for success with this candle is time.

How to – dip and carve candle

EQUIPMENT AND MATERIALS
Thermometer; craft knife; three to five dipping cans containing wax of different colours at 85°C (185°F); white spirit; 20cm (8in) length of 5cm (2in) wick.

Simple dip and carve candle.

METHOD

1. Dip the wick just over half-way into one of the colours and hold it there for three seconds. Lift the wick up, allow it to cool for twenty seconds, then remove the wax from the lower part of the wick with your fingers. Repeat this to build up a plum-sized ball of wax in the centre of the wick. Allow it to cool for two minutes.

2. Choose a different colour and, by repeatedly dipping and cleaning the lower part of the wick, increase the diameter of the ball by about 2.5cm (1in). Allow it to cool.

3. Repeat the process with further colours until the ball of wax is about the size of an orange. Hang it up to cool for at least five hours.

4. Carve back through the wax to reveal the sequence of colours beneath. You can then polish the exposed surfaces with white spirit. Allow this to evaporate fully, then buff the candle with a wet tissue.

Building up a ball of wax in the centre of the wick.

Peeled banana

Dip and carve can be used to produce an attractive novelty candle that is a great favourite with children. The peeled banana candle was invented by Essex candlemaker Frances Fell. Her candles were entirely handmade and required considerable skill to get the texture of the fruit. My version uses a moulded fruit and can be made by beginners.

The candle is made in two stages. The inner fruit is cast in a 'banana fruit' flexible mould, and the skin is added by dipping it in dip and carve wax. This dipping is itself a two-stage process with an inner and an outer layer.

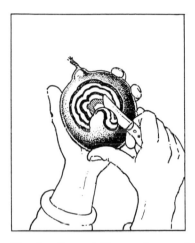

Carving through the wax to reveal the colours beneath.

How to – peeled banana candles

EQUIPMENT AND MATERIALS

Double boiler; thermometer; dipping cans; banana fruit flexible mould; wicking needle; cardboard mould collar; mirror; craft knife; 500g (1lb 2oz) paraffin wax; 5kg (11lb) dip and carve wax; 19g (approx. 1 disc) yellow dye; 11.84g (approx. ⅗ disc) cream dye; 37.35g (approx. 1⅘ discs) chalky white dye; 2.5g (1⁄12 oz) Vybar; six 25cm (10in) lengths of 2.5cm (1in) wick. These materials are sufficient to make six candles.

METHOD – FRUIT

1. Melt 500g (1lb 2oz) paraffin wax and add 1.24g (approx. 1⁄20 disc) cream dye, 3.75g (approx. ⅕ disc) chalky white dye, and 2.5g (1⁄12 oz) Vybar.

2. Wick up the mould and support it with a stiff cardboard collar. Pour in the wax at 93°C (199°F).

3. As the wax cools, use a wicking needle to keep the surface

Peeled banana candles made by the dip and carve method.

broken at the top; this prevents the mould from distorting as the wax shrinks.

4. Handle the finished fruit as little as possible to avoid spoiling the surface texture.

METHOD – SKIN

This is applied in two layers, but there should be no appreciable delay between layers. Prepare both lots of wax before you start dipping. For the inner layer you will require 2.5kg (5lb 8oz) dip and carve wax, 7.5g (approx. ⅜ disc) yellow dye, and 28g (approx. 1⅖ discs) chalky white dye. The outer layer requires 2.5kg (5lb 8oz) dip and carve wax, 11.5g (approx. ⅗ disc) yellow dye, 10.6g (approx. ½ disc) cream dye, and 5.6g (approx. ¼ disc) chalky white dye. If you wish to make larger or smaller quantities, then make sure that you alter the quantities of dye in exact proportion.

1. Maintain the temperature of the wax in the dipping cans at 65°C (149°F).

2. Firstly, dip the moulded candle into cold water. Shake off any excess water, but do not wipe the candle.

3. Quickly dip the candle in and out of the 'inner' mix. Wait for one minute.

4. Give the candle another eight dips, each of just less than one second, with about one minute between dips.

5. After the last dip in the 'inner' mix, wait for one minute and then start dipping in the 'outer' mix. Again, each dip should be just less than one second, with a short interval between dips. A good way to judge the interval is to wait for the yellow dye to darken as it cools.

6. Around ten to twelve dips will give the right thickness of skin. After the final dip, allow the candle to cool for about five minutes. Press the sides of the candle against a smooth surface, such as a mirror, to give the banana its distinctive squared-off appearance.

7. With a craft knife, make four vertical cuts through the skin, down to within 4cm (1½in) of the base. Start each cut on the wick, and use only moderate pressure.

8. Then, peel your banana just like a real fruit, arrange the flaps of peel, and allow the candle to cool completely before handling.

Cutting corners

Joe Tannetta is a British candlemaker who makes beautiful candles. He is an accomplished master of one particular application of dip and carve, that is, cutting into the candle and peeling back the cut wax like the petals of a flower.

This technique works only when the candle has been covered with several layers of dip and carve wax. The resins in the dip and carve wax make it pliable when warm, yet it cools to a hard, shiny finish. The secrets of success lie in timing and temperature, that is, letting the wax cool for exactly the right amount of time and then working swiftly whilst the wax is at the optimum carving temperature.

The technique can be used on any candle of regular symmetrical shape, e.g. cylindrical, rectangular, or hexagonal. At the beginning, you may find it easier to confine yourself to shapes that have well-defined corners which are easy to cut.

How to – basic techniques

EQUIPMENT AND MATERIALS

Thermometer; dipping cans (one for water); small sharp knife; loops of stiff wire; one core candle of suitable shape with an extra long wick at the top; several colours of dip and carve wax (enough of each colour to dip your candle).

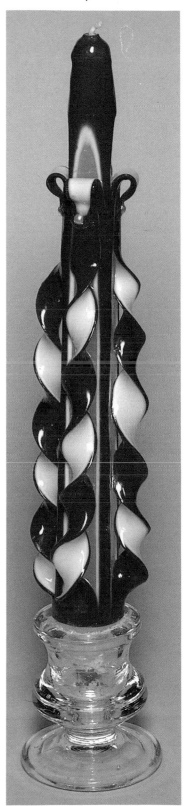

Cut and curl taper.

Star-moulded candles with cut and curl corners.

METHOD – DIPPING

1. Melt the dip and carve waxes and heat them to 74°C (165°F).

2. Dip the core candle into the first colour of dip and carve wax and hold it there for thirty seconds. This softens the outer surface.

3. Dip the candle in and out of the cold water. Wipe off any drops of water with your hand.

4. Dip the candle into the dip and carve wax for three seconds, then dip it in and out of cold water. Wipe off any drops of water.

5. Repeat this at least three times, then change colours. Three dips gives a narrow band of colour, whilst ten dips gives a fairly wide band. Remember to dip in and out of cold water between each dip into wax.

6. Hang the candle by its wick, and trim the drips from the base to leave a level surface so that the candle will stand upright.

7. You must start cutting within four to five minutes of the final dip. You then have only twelve to fifteen minutes in which to work, so plan your design carefully.

METHOD – CUT AND CURL CORNERS

1. Make the first cut about 5cm (2in) from the base, and cut down at a narrow angle to within about 2cm (¾ in) of the base.
2. As you remove the knife, bend the wax back slightly.
3. With your fingers, bend the wax back and curl it round.
4. Rotate the candle and repeat the process on the other corners.
5. When you have gone right around the candle, start another layer of curls above the first. When bent back, the curls should almost touch. Repeat for further layers.
6. For an attractive 'overhang' effect, make your final cuts from the top edge of the candle.
7. For variation, curls can be bent to one side, cut vertically and then pulled apart, or formed into complex orchid shapes.

METHOD – SPIRALS

1. A rectangular candle can be greatly enhanced by a dramatic spiral at each corner. Make a continuous almost vertical cut down each corner, twist the wax into a spiral, then pinch the top of the spiral to the top of the candle.
2. Spirals can be inserted into the face of a candle by using gouge or loop wire to cut a groove and curl of wax. Twist the curl into a spiral and then gently press it back into the groove.
3. You can also use gouges to cut flower designs into the sides of a candle.

Star-moulded candles with cut and curl corners.

Snake on a branch.

Coiled snake candle.

Snakes

Werner Muhlenberg is a German candlemaker who produces astonishingly realistic reptiles. Looped lazily over the limbs of trees, or coiled on the ground ready to strike, his snakes represent imaginative candlemaking at its best.

I went to Germany to meet the master in his candlemaking den, and one of his conditions to seeing me was that some of his trade secrets should remain secret. One of these was the blend of waxes that he has perfected. If you want to experiment, then I do not think that I am being unfair to Herr Muhlenberg if I suggest that you use uncoloured dip and carve wax. For the same reason, I cannot give you step-by-step instructions. Instead, I will describe the stages in the process.

Wax is poured out on to a baking tray to form a sheet about 2cm (¾ in) thick. When the wax is rubbery all the way through, it is painted with several layers of contrasting colours, e.g. black, white, and yellow. Each layer is flamed with a gas torch before the next is applied. The sheet of wax is then taken from the tray, and the surface is scored with a saw blade to make diamond-shaped scales. A 5cm (2in) strip is then cut from the sheet, and the edges turned inward. The head is shaped, the tail trimmed, and the body rolled into a cylinder which is then flattened slightly. Glass dolls' eyes are fitted, and the snake is then draped over a pre-cast log or stone.

Snake on a rock.

NOVELTY CANDLES

Novelty candles

Whatever the end product, a simple dipped candle or a multi-layered landscape, candlemaking is always an enjoyable experience. There is something deeply satisfying about the smell of hot wax and the alchemical combination of ingredients, timing, and temperature.

In this final section, I have collected together a number of different techniques which greatly extend the scope of creative candlemaking. For want of a better word, I call them novelty candles because they are an ideal way of celebrating both large and small occasions – a loved one's birthday, a children's party, or one of those wonderful afternoons when you have the time and the inclination to create something really special.

In most cases I give detailed instructions for making one particular candle, but do not be afraid to adapt, experiment, or create your own entirely new designs.

Whipped wax candles

As it cools, liquid wax can be beaten or whipped into a froth like the white of an egg. The easiest method is to use an old kitchen fork. Whipped wax behaves rather like whipped cream and can be sculpted into gravity-defying shapes. Whipped wax has the added advantage of setting hard at room temperature. The cooled wax has an attractive surface texture which can be exploited to good effect.

How to – ice-cream cone

EQUIPMENT AND MATERIALS
Double boiler; fork; dessertspoon; 100g (3½ oz) paraffin wax; red dye; triangular piece of beeswax sheet with sides measuring 12.5cm (5in).

METHOD
1. Roll the piece of beeswax sheet into a cone and pinch the seam closed.
2. Melt the paraffin wax and remove it from the heat. Once a skin has formed, beat it with a fork until it is stiff, then spoon it on to the top of the cone and shape it as desired. A trickle of wax dyed bright red can provide a touch of mouth-watering strawberry topping.

A mouth-watering ice-cream candle, with a chocolate flake made from strips of brown modelling wax. The wax hand has been cast from the author's own hand.

Birthday cake candles

Parents, partners, and professional pastry-cooks often spend a great deal of time and trouble decorating thematic birthday cakes, e.g. an electric guitar, a cricket pitch, the green at the 16th hole, and so on. With a little imagination and creative endeavour, you can create candles to enhance almost any commemorative cake. Whatever the end product, you make the basic candle by dipping (see pages 16–18). Use a fine grade of wick, such as 1.25cm (½in), because you are only making very small candles. Various methods can be used for shaping them.

• Selective dipping produces blobs on the end that can be pressed into the heads of golf clubs.
• Pulling the candle between your thumb and two fingers produces a cricket bat with the authentic V-shaped back.
• Pressing the upper part of the candle flat and trimming it to shape can produce a tennis racket or a guitar.

Once cool, the candles can be painted with coloured wax to add further detail (see page 56).

Balloon candles

This is a tricky technique, but worth taking the time and trouble to master. It produces lovely round candles with a translucent surface over swirls of bright colour. As you experiment, you will learn a lot about the physical properties of wax, especially its strengths and weaknesses.

Balloon candles involve very thin shells of wax, and even experts break a few now and then. The shells can also be deformed by holding them too firmly or for too long in warm hands. Once you have dented a shell, the dent is impossible to remove. Working in the airstream of an electric fan helps to keep the shells cool and firm.

How to – balloon candle

EQUIPMENT AND MATERIALS
Double boiler; thermometer; four teaspoons and a tablespoon; egg poacher; wicking needle; 1kg (2lb 3oz) paraffin wax; four contrasting dyes; 12.5cm (5in) length of 5cm (2in) wick; balloon that forms a suitable shape when partly filled with water.

METHOD
1. Melt the wax and heat it to 82°C (180°F).
2. Pour small quantities of wax into the egg poacher, dye them, and keep them liquid.
3. Fill the balloon with water until it is about 10cm (4in) in diameter. Hold the neck tightly closed, and dry the balloon thoroughly with a tissue.

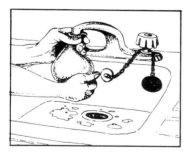

Filling the balloon with water.

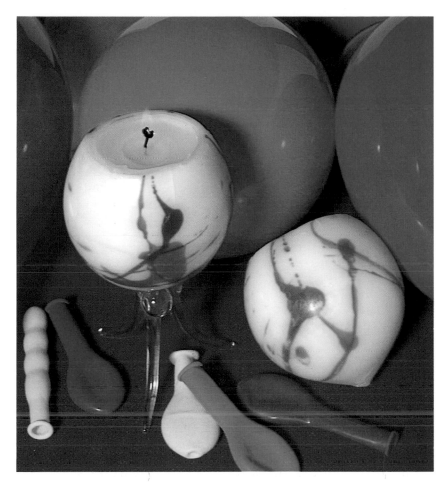

Dipping the balloon into the wax.

Removing the water from the balloon.

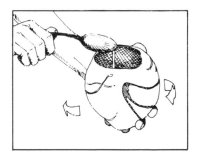

Spooning dye into the wax shell.

Filling the wicked-up candle shell with wax.

4. Dip the balloon into the wax ten times, allowing thirty seconds between dips. Working with only six dips gives a better result, but it is very difficult to do because the wax is so thin.

5. Carefully let the water out of the balloon, and gently remove the balloon from the wax shell.

6. Spoon small amounts of dye into the shell and swirl them around the inside. As you work, blow into the shell to cool the dye.

7. When you have laid down sufficient colour, begin to fill the shell with undyed wax using the tablespoon. Add one spoonful of wax at a time and swirl it around the inner surface. Pour any excess back into the double boiler. Slowly build up layers of wax until the shell is about 1.25cm (½ in) thick.

8. Prime the wick and, with the wicking needle, carefully thread the wick down through the top of the shell. Attach the wick as with moulded candles (see page 31), taking care not to damage the wax shell.

9. Fill the candle with wax one tablespoon at a time, allowing each spoonful to set and cool before adding the next.

10. Allow the finished candle to cool for one hour before buffing the surface with a wet tissue.

Sand candles

These represent creative candlemaking at its very best – creating beautiful candles from shapeless sand and raw wax. For sheer flickering, glowing beauty, nothing can compare with a sand candle as the light soaks through the outer layer of sand. Try one and I think you will agree with me.

Sand candles are very simple. An impression is made in wet sand, and then this is used as a mould to cast a candle. Depending upon the temperature of the wax, it will seep some distance into the sand, creating a crusty coating that can be shaped and carved by hand. Because the sand mould is used only once, you are not limited to shapes that can be lifted cleanly out of the mould. If you can get the shape to stay in damp sand, then you can cast it in wax. Different grades of sand provide different textures and colours. Use as little water as is necessary to get the sand to stay in shape. Generally, 140cm^3 (¼pt) of water to half a bucket of dry sand is about right.

The instructions that follow are a guide to one particular candle, but they can be varied as you wish, for example, as in the star-shaped candles shown above. The important point to remember is that the hotter the wax, the more it will seep into the sand.

Packing the damp sand around the wooden block.

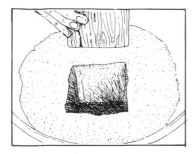

Removing the wood from the sand.

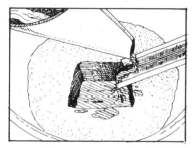

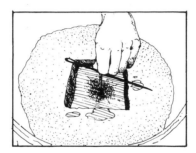

Pouring the wax over the thermometer into the sand mould.

Inserting the wick.

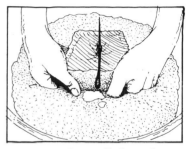

Removing the candle from the sand.

How to – sand candle

EQUIPMENT AND MATERIALS

Saucepan; thermometer; long wicking needle; pair of dividers for marking out design; surface-forming tool or rasp; carving tools; electric iron; block of wood 20 × 7.5 × 7.5cm (8 × 3 × 3in); 2kg (4lb 6oz) paraffin wax containing 1 per cent beeswax; yellow dye; 24cm (9½ in) length of 5cm (2in) wick; half a bucket of damp sand.

METHOD

1. Put a 7.5cm (3in) layer of sand in the bottom of the bucket, and place the block of wood centrally on top of it. Pack the rest of the sand around the wooden block, then tap the bucket sharply on the floor to pack the sand firmly.
2. Remove the wood from the sand, taking care not to knock any sand from the sides. If you are not happy with the impression, then start again.
3. Melt and dye the wax and carefully heat it to 127°C (261°F). Pour the wax over the thermometer into the mould, trying to disturb the sand as little as possible.
4. After about three minutes the wax will have seeped into the sand. Refill the mould with wax at 127°C (261°F) and allow it to cool.
5. After two hours, a well will form. Push the wicking needle down through the centre and insert the primed wick. Top up the well with wax at 104°C (219°F) and allow it to cool.
6. After five hours, remove the candle from the sand. (Because a water bath cannot be used, sand candles take much longer to cool than other candles.)
7. With the surface-forming tool or rasp, remove the excess sand and roughly shape the candle.
8. Mark out the design with the dividers and scratch it into the surface.
9. Carve out the design, then round off the end of the candle with an iron set on a medium heat.

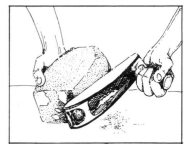

Removing the excess sand.

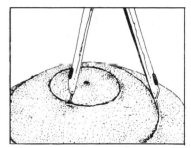

Marking out the design.

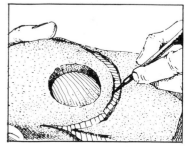

Carving out the design.

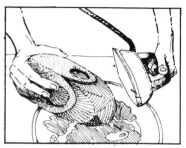

Rounding off the candle.

73

Water candles

These are quite difficult to make and you will need plenty of practice before you can exert any real influence over the outcome. However, the results can be spectacular – delicate fronds of feathery wax rising from a central core. Because water candles are always somewhat unpredictable, each time that you take the plunge there is the chance of a quite unexpectedly attractive result.

Water candles rely on the fact that wax floats. Hot wax is drawn through cold water, and as the wax rises to the surface it cools and becomes frozen in place. The best results are obtained using specially blended water candle wax and it is not really worth trying this technique with ordinary wax. Always wear rubber gloves when making water candles, as prolonged contact with hot wax at these temperatures will burn your fingers.

How to – water candles

EQUIPMENT AND MATERIALS

There are two closely related methods – plunge and pour – both of which require similar materials and equipment. Double boiler; thermometer; tank of water at least 30cm (12in) deep; rubber gloves; saucer (plunge method only); pouring jug (pour method only); 500g (1lb 2oz) water candle wax; dipped candle 20cm (8in) long and 1.8cm (¾in) in diameter.

METHOD – PLUNGE

1. Melt the wax and heat it to 93°C (199°F).
2. Fix a dipped candle to the centre of a saucer, either by melting the end or by using wax glue.
3. Fill the saucer with hot wax, then plunge it into the water, twisting it round as you do so.
4. If you are unhappy with the result, then the water candle wax can be melted down and used again. Please take care when remelting the wax, in case any water has become trapped. If the water is allowed to boil, then it will sputter badly.

METHOD – POUR

1. Melt 80g (3oz) of the wax and pour it into a disc shape, 10cm (4in) in diameter and 6mm (¼in) thick. Allow it to cool.
2. Melt the remainder of the wax and heat it to 93°C (199°F).
3. Stick the dipped candle to the centre of the wax disc, and transfer the hot wax to a suitable pouring jug.
4. Holding the edge of the disc at an angle against the surface of the water, pour wax on to the lower edge of the disc.
5. Whilst continuing to pour, push the disc smoothly down and round into the water. A small pool of wax will form on the surface. Continue to pour wax into this pool until that branch of the candle is sufficiently high.
6. Repeat the procedure at other points on the edge of the disc.

Plunge method

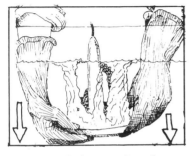

Plunging the hot wax into the water.

Pour method

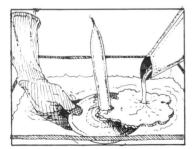

Pouring the hot wax on to the candle disc.

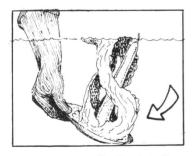

Pushing the candle disc into the water.

Filling the mould with broken ice.

Pouring the wax over the ice.

Ice candles

This is a simple technique that is perfect for introducing children to the mysteries of liquids and solids. You start and finish with solid wax and liquid water, but during the candlemaking process you use liquid wax and solid water. Ice candles work because wax forms a skin when it cools. Contact with the ice freezes the wax into shape before the heat of the wax melts the ice. The result is a candle with holes where the ice used to be.

How to – ice candle

EQUIPMENT AND MATERIALS

Double boiler; thermometer; cylindrical mould; bowl; 450g (1lb) paraffin wax; brightly coloured dye; 1.25cm (½in) diameter candle cut to the same length as the mould; ice broken into 1–2cm (½–¾in) chunks.

METHOD

1. Melt and dye the wax, and heat it to 99°C (210°F).
2. Use the 1.25cm (½in) candle as a wick and insert it into the mould. Make sure that the wick of the candle goes through the hole in the end. Do not use mould seal, as you will want the water to run out.
3. Stand the mould in a bowl and fill it with broken ice, taking care not to disturb the wick candle.
4. With one constant flow, pour the wax over the ice, filling the mould.
5. Leave it to cool for one hour and dry the candle thoroughly before lighting it.

Burning down

A well-balanced candle will burn evenly with a smokeless flame, without producing any excess melted wax to drip or gutter from the candle.

- A candle should be at least a day old before burning.
- Candles should not be burnt in a draught.
- The wick should be trimmed to 1–2cm (½–¾in) in length.

When a finished candle fails to burn well, there is usually a traceable reason, assuming that you followed carefully all the steps in making it. Listed here are some of the most common burning problems, the probable reasons for them, and what best to do about them.

Dripping.

Small flame.

Smoking.

Drowning wick.

BURNING FLAW	CAUSE	WHAT TO DO
Dripping	Draughts.	Keep candle out of draughts.
	Wax too soft.	Check proportions of wax mixture. Use harder wax, or plastic additive.
	Wick poorly positioned or too small.	Use a larger wick.
Candle will not burn	Wick unprimed.	Hold candle upside-down and light it.
	Mould seal on wick.	Try to clean off mould seal.
	Water on wick.	Try to dry wick.
Small flame	Wax may be too hard. Wick too small. Wick clogged with pigment or dust in candle.	Check wax mixture. Use a larger wick. Use wax dyes rather than insoluble pigments, and keep wax free of dust.
Smoking	Draughts.	Keep candle out of draughts.
	Flame not oxidizing well; wick too large.	Trim wick, or use a smaller one.
Wick burns in too small a diameter	Wax too hard. Wick too small.	Check wax mixture, or use a larger wick.
Wick drowns itself in molten wax	Wick too small.	Use a larger wick or softer wax.
	Wick seated too loosely in candle.	Improve tension of the wick when wicking up the mould.
	Insoluble pigments used instead of wax dyes.	
Sputtering prevalent with ice and water candles	Water in or around wick.	Pour off pool of wax around the wick and relight candle. If it still sputters, then remelt it or throw it away.

Faults

Listed here are some of the common problems likely to be encountered when making dipped and moulded candles, the probable reasons for them, and what best to do about them.

DIPPING

FAULT	CAUSE	WHAT TO DO
Lumpy surface on candle	First dip too fast. Wax too cold whilst dipping.	Whilst candle is still warm, roll it on a smooth surface.
Candle spits whilst burning	Water in candle.	Pour off molten wax and relight candle. If this is not successful, then remelt it.
White marks in layers of dip and iron back candles	Wax too cold whilst dipping.	A quick dip in wax at 93°C (199°F) may be successful.
Candle cracks whilst plaiting or rolling	Uneven temperature throughout candle, i.e. the centre may be harder than the surface of the candle.	Re-dip candle until pliable.
Scum forms on the surface when floating wax on water	Impurities or dirty wax.	Ladle off scum. Make sure that you still have 3.8cm (1½in) of molten wax.
Damaged or old candle	Age, dirt, fading, etc.	Rub over surface with nylon stocking and white spirit. Decorate to cover flaws.

CASTING IN MOULDS

FAULT	CAUSE	WHAT TO DO
Air bubbles on surface	Poured too fast. Placed in water bath too soon. Dust in mould. Mould not tapped to remove air.	Pour slowly. Wait for one minute before placing in water bath. Clean mould. Tap mould one minute after pouring.
Seepage between candle and mould	Wax allowed to set and contract away from the side of the mould, allowing some of the topping-up wax to seep down the side.	Cut off the unwanted marks.
Loss of definition with a layered candle	Previously poured wax not set sufficiently to support the next layer. The surface should be rubbery.	Remelt. Remember that the resulting wax will be a combination of colours, usually brown.
Layers not joining	Wax poured too late or at too low a temperature.	Remelt.
Misshapen candle; sides caved in	Surface around wick not broken and probed soon enough. Air in centre of candle.	Keep surface constantly broken until candle is almost set.
Soap-like appearance	Too much stearin added.	Check proportion of wax mixture.
Candle will not come out of mould	Not enough stearin added. Candle topped up above the original level, causing seepage between candle and mould. Cooling too slow, resulting in insufficient contraction.	Place in hot water and melt candle out of mould. Alternatively, place in refrigerator for twenty minutes.
Ring of discolouration around top of candle	Dirty wax.	Take more care. Keep moulds and utensils clean.
Scaly marks on surface	Wax poured too cold for prevailing room temperature.	Use a water bath. Pour at a higher temperature.
Mould leaking from base	Careless wicking up. Damaged mould.	Seal with mould seal. Place candle in water bath immediately.
Small bubbly line encircling candle	Mark of water-level from water bath. Water added after candle placed in bath.	Rub with nylon stocking. Fill water bath almost to top of mould level before putting mould in.
Cracks throughout candle	Candle allowed to become too cold before topping up.	Use water bath at room temperature.

Index